Anchor

Anchor

poems

Rebecca Aronson

ISBN: 978-1-949039-35-1

Orison Books
PO Box 8385
Asheville, NC 28814
www.orisonbooks.com

Distributed to the trade by Itasca Books
(952) 223-8373 / orders@itascabooks.com

Cover Art: Photograph of original illustration from "A System of Human Anatomy" by Erasmus Wilson, published in 1859. Image courtesy of iStock.

Manufactured in the U.S.A.

ORISON
BOOKS

In memoriam Donald G. and Claire S. Aronson

and for Nancy

CONTENTS

Bushy:
Each substance of a grief hath twenty shadows,
Which shows like grief itself, but is not so;
For sorrow's eye, glazed with blinding tears,
Divides one thing entire to many objects,
. . .

    —Shakespeare, *Richard the Second*, Act II, Scene ii

Gravity is a habit that is hard to shake off.
    —Terry Pratchett, *Small Gods*

DEAR GRAVITY,

May I call you Grave? An old tree falls
after long weakening, after years of unseen hollowing,
and it keeps falling, rotted core turning to damp dust,
becoming earth. The body its own trench.
At the doctor's office, the nurse says
I've grown shorter. *Only natural.* I stare hard
but can't wipe the pleasant smile off her face.
I am sinking not quite like a ship or a deflating balloon,
but like the house's foundation. I am the house
and the clay it is built on and eventually
the unrecognizable ruin. My mother's hips
are out of plumb; she lists like a sailboat
about to slice sideways into waves and then under.
My father's head is even with my own, so he's winning
the shrinking race. Imagine us becoming not just shorter
but thinner, not lying down for a last time
but disappearing altogether, like a popsicle
that has melted into a stain on someone's smile.

SAN STEFANO

It won't be the cancer that kills you, the doctor said. And it was and it wasn't
but while you lived with it inside you it was the cancer that consumed
the space of your worry. At San Stefano we walked through the Sette Chiese
at different paces, you slow with your cane, leaning toward every plaque and niche
and me, faster, circling past and back, a goldfish revisiting a pretty castle.
The brochure told the story and you
told the story but I didn't really care about the story;
I wanted mainly to look at the way the light falling through an arch
changes the mossy stubble on the ancient bricks
from glistening paint to a dull stain
according to the hour.
What I love is the dark that pools
in a courtyard corner and how those small cars sometimes careen
through the late afternoon hush sending pigeons whirring,
their maraca wings rattling the sky. I got up the nerve
to ask how you felt about dying
and you told me and we went for gelato again.

THE LAST FALLING

Won't be over the ragged edge
of Vesuvius, preceded by your wind-stolen hat
swirling out of reach, nor into the jeweled décolletage
of a dance partner, though it might be
on the swath of damp yard
that snakes along the roadway—
the boundary of your last home—
as you navigate with cane and grocery bag
and keys. You will, like a man swooning,
dip fast the sack of your body,
needing only gravity. And my arms,
lacking the gym muscles of a good son,
nonetheless will be up
to a desperate task:
a smatter of seconds and grace to
will your head cradled
above the puddle, the asphalt, above breaking.
Or it will occur in sleep,
yours or mine,
and I will miss it and never know
the exact angle.

DEAR GRAVITY,

Do you imagine he is trying to escape you? Jealous, you pull him close
and closer. Leave cement kisses on his appendages. His blood soaks
through asphalt, through sidewalk paving, pools in car parks
trying to get to you. Already you are bonded. See, he loves you
back. Only his bones, they might belong to air.
It's not so much they strive for flight, but they dissolve,
becoming mist, becoming cloud. His heavy brain
unbalances him. I know, you are trying to make an anchor,
having filled his legs with fluid until they nearly burst.
Hear them sloshing. I think they have their own tides
that tug and wash him to the ground
which embraces him the only way it knows; armless and inarticulate,
it can only bruise. You want him all to yourself
but he is half floating, half falling, stretched between realms.
You yearn for his attention, pull with such insistence
he begins to split, beloved toy you have adored to pieces.

TOURIST

We stayed once above a plaza so filled with noise
sleep hovered in the room's corners
like a nervy hummingbird. Halfway across
stood a severe statue, memorial
of a story I only ever half-remembered.
In new cities I am always partway lost, navigate by fountain
and luck. I am no magnet. My dreams too
lead me only halfway to desire. I yearn
or yell and the dream slips around like a loose shell.
Here is some of what I have held: baby bird, unbroken
but half dead; dying mice; the hot hands
of half-grown children; my own want
which beats counter-point in the veins of my wrist.
You live in your head, my friend
who sculpts bodies for a living says.
Half true. In those weeks I only half slept
and so I was only ever partly conscious, moving
through that unfamiliar landscape
as a ghost might, wishing to touch every beautiful thing
but unable to recall what any of it was for.

TABLEAU

Because I never saw the butcher lift even one skinned rabbit
from the line hung in the window, I did not consider

that somewhere up the road was a crowded hutch
in which they huddled. I did not picture the soft ears laid flat

while a hand groped into the straw-dusted recesses.
Nor did I, as I might expect, allow the image of steam rising from a shallow dish

or those slim flanks braised on a plate with parsley sprigs and spring potatoes. I
    looked
at the rabbit-shaped bodies suspended on silver hooks

in the clear shelf of the frame, the pane wiped clean I guess
each evening, and the sun bright on the glass

in which was reflected the wispy boulevard trees just now blossoming
above the passers by, and saw across the street three blue awnings

blurred with sky, their flapping
like a flash of something disappearing fast into tall grasses.

CLIMATE CHANGE

All winter, rosebuds
burst and wither on the wilding bush
climbing the walls and front window,
death and re-birth a weekly show
endlessly recycling as the weather's
Ferris wheel rolls high to low,
going so quickly my head
halves and echoes. I can't keep up with anything,
I tell the hamster in his colorful
jail. He's gnawing at what
keeps him safe. His teeth are
lit and sparking: metal kernels,
molten planetary cores. Let
night flash by sweat-filled and sinister,
oily waves of it, time crashing as
people always said it would. This
quagmire of change, middle age
roiling my body's careless army:
surrender on any terms, surrender terminally,
total and predetermined.
Unsurprisingly, we are back at death.
Variously stubborn, radiant, afraid, I am daily undone:
world news with its dosages of fear-porn,
xenophobic ramblings, post-post-modern anguish…
yet the rosebuds slay me;
zygotes of the coming world, its foreseeable blooming.

DEAR GRAVITY,

Shall I call you Shiva? I know your pleasures:
taking down an overpass, toppling a crane.
You downed a space shuttle for its presumption. Flick
at people as we scuttle. You pulled me down once
to test my brittle frame. You win. My bones are balsa
and they bend only a little. It was just a prank, your attention
really elsewhere. Class bully, you're picking on another nerd
whose limbs stiffen like drying plaster. The rest of him
is air, except his head, so full he can hardly balance.
In there, he holds the secrets of your might
and functions. You can't abide a mind that knows you well,
so once again, you knock my father to the ground.

CHRYSANTHEMUM

Before they rot and darken orange, chrysanthemum feathers spin onto the table like twirling skirts, silky as cat ears and temporary. As everything. Only more so. The cat's nubby tongue is solid like a word like oligarchy but it is only a petal disintegrating. Even the swirly glass paperweight, lead-heavy, is a petal: my breath, your hand, petals which would smear to nothing in a good rain, a hard melt. Petal civilization, petal walls, petal generations marking a single planet a little for a little while, petal in space, starlight already gone—reclining on a lawn chair to fix the sight into your petal eyes won't make it less gone, won't laminate the petal of your life which is brief, which is delicate and weightier than you know.

LATCH

My hand in the dark on the lump in my breast, right
where the needle made its bite,

where I used to ask a friend to help me
fasten a cameo straight

on my favorite blue dress,
the one with the front buttons

that came undone if you looked at them
too long. I floated

in midnight lakes, pale areolae
in star-flecked water, everyone's wet

skin moonlit and fantastic.
I flashed a man who wouldn't stop staring

at the shape of my chest under my waitress uniform.
There were hours spent fixed

in place while the late afternoon swooned dark
and the baby sucked and fought sleep,

his mouth on the swollen nipple,
a milk drop pearled on his lip

when he finally let go. Yes,
I bound them and hid them

in jogging bras, under loose sweaters and formless dresses,
wanted them smaller for a better silhouette, a smooth

line an eye could glide past
without a snag,

then spilled them over bikini tops
which untied as I dove, but

mostly I did not think of them. A body
is a just a set of nerves in fur and spangles.

A shopping cart
with one disobedient wheel. But now

here I am in the vast new country
where fear lives, the tender island in my breast,

clutching a scribble of creases, this map
of tributaries, but no roads.

DEAR GRAVITY,

At night I think about you just as I think about the moon,
how it pulls my body's rhythms into shapes
I live by but never asked for. You dislodge
an old man from his own center, my father
subverted. You and the moon meddle and distort.
I want to understand, as if knowledge were actually power.
Things fall because space curves. Space curves because of matter.
The body's matter displaces space a little with every step,
and so he falls, my father, his mind on the curve
of pavement, carefully treading on matter's ghostly shadow.

THE DRESS I LOVED

had a ribboned hem and vertical stripes
where light flowed through. Wearing it

I was a grove of shadowed birch, a waterfall's scattered refraction,
a vine growing out of the hard wall of a mesa.

Explorers asking the way to the City of Gold
Casino believed I was pointing them

in the right direction. At parties the dress became guardian
of the names of secret lovers and unsayable desires.

When I walked the dress to work, the sidewalk sidled alongside
bumping my leg like a needful dog. If I allowed a hand to follow

the long spine of the zipper, my shoulders slid like lake stones,
blades blurring as if rain, as if a forest turning night. The dress was never tight

no matter how many particles I swallowed. When I wore it
my face became like the memory of a face, unfixed

but probably smiling. The dress was a year of seconds,
a hill made of spears of grass that slight breezes

kept undoing. The dress was a wish I made as a child,
the one my tongue held long after the ripples around the splash subsided.

IS THAT ALL THERE IS?

I used to hip-check the jukebox
when I passed it if I didn't like the song playing;
the music would veer and skip where my curve met
the rounded corner of neon and metal. I took out Peggy Lee's guttural whine
this way every month until they finally stopped replacing it.
I looked good in my stain-hiding brown waitress uniform,
shined up with kitchen heat and magnetic.
I wanted to dance because dancing made a flame
lick at the edges of everything. Here was the secret
to living: what is dull can be polished
to a hot glow with the right friction.
What is lost can be added to the heart's altar.
Peggy Lee wailed her faith in disappointment
but she was wrong:
even the fryer grease
that hung in the air and followed me
from work to the bar
once made a hungry boy tell me
I smelled miraculous.

MY MOTHER DISAPPROVES

of afternoon languor, lying on couches,
textured wallpaper. Hammocks; guest rooms
in which the fold-out bed is left unfolded.
Curtains left closed past eight or open
past dark. Matinees, drive-ins, daytime television.
Snacking, sweet cocktails, state fairs. Corn dogs, hotdogs, dogs,
any talk of god. Dive bars. Motorcycles, mini-skirts,
pleather. Cartoons, line dancing. Most music
composed past the eighteenth century. Day-drinking, playing hooky, ganja,
and boy bands. Camping. Car trips, RVs, Christmas lights.
Orange soda. Messy rooms. Spell check, tube tops. Arrows
drawn through a heart or shot
at a bullseye.
Drama, melodrama, melancholy, snakes. Cigarettes,
green cars, mistletoe, skinny-dipping. A smoky eye,
tight pants, my uncombed hair,
the fleshy, unbound hours of my every day and night.

MY MOTHER AT THE GATE

After only a few minutes I lose my cool. I swear
by my left foot I'll last longer,
count to ten or twenty and breathe both in *and* out. I offer
deals: help me to say only pleasant things in a quiet voice,
etc. and I will…and here it falls apart. What would I do?
Forgo wine on weeknights? Live broke, as I do, but
gratefully? Whatever. Just grant me patience,
hospitable syntax, and the outward demeanor of gentility.
I consider meditation, therapy, more and more yoga.
Just in time I crack a joke, which sometimes helps. Sometimes
kindness descends like a fever. We walk the halls
laughing at nonsense and are briefly cheerful.
My mother loved me once and knows it still. She recalls
nothing of my childhood and next to nothing of hers;
ordinary tasks are either hard-wired into her hands (the coffee
pot placed on the counter by the stove, the toaster oven set to medium. She writes
questions to ask later on a pad on the counter)—or wiped into an un-
readable blur. She squints as if trying to decipher her own mind
scrawled inscrutably just there. We all know memory is a farce, but still
this blankness galls. She *knows* in moments and feels I'd guess despair.
Until I became a mother I lacked imagination. Motherhood shot me into
vertigo, the endless falling and fear of failing, and goddamnit,
wonder. I think of the delicate silver chain she gave me once:
xoxo across the front, a talisman to carry me through
years, but no one thought to prepare—or thought but had no means,
zero instructions ever coming close—for this third rail of oblivion.

SHELL

Not pearls for the wedding. Not bone
China, delicate as sand dollars. Not the set
of encyclopedia nor the hours curled
in the corner of the flax-colored couch
slowly thumbing onion-skin pages. Not the swirling carpet
sun-lit to a blazing blur in the afternoons, the curtains
translucent flames winging the windows in that hour.
Not the hour, with the hall clock's magnifying tick, the house
like the inside of an egg, the yolk of daylight,
and outside, the softening snowbanks under which the season
fermented.
                You who mothered me. Who looked too closely
or looked away entirely. Who looked
but could not decipher what you saw. The whispering girl
tightly twisting the phone cord. The boyfriends,
the bills lifted from your wallet. What I wore
and what you said about it. All of the words. My brother's hat
at the dinner table. The echo after a slammed door. Our clandestine leavings
and late returns. Never saying where we were really going
no matter how benign.
                Look at me
litigating what now never was.
Now that the stories
have no before or after, they blaze
brief and bright as flashbulbs
and go dark.

IN THESE DAYS BEFORE

My mother tastes whatever she is given
without comment. She drinks
only a little water, only a little wine,
and only if it is poured into a tiny glass and set
directly in front of her.
Whose drink is this, she'll say, *I never asked for this.*
And who could argue,
even with the beveled facets
shining in good light,
whatever liquid inside the glass
glowing like something Vermeer painted?
What could recover the memory
of thirst?

DEAR GRAVITY,

My bones are hollow. I dream of flight.
In dreams I am not afraid
to look down. You are my uncle
a thousand times removed. There's a family resemblance,
they say, as I am aging my way to ground.
Someday maybe I'll be a stump
the other birds pause to rest on.
What is finer than *am*? Not *was*. Not *was*.

UNDERNEATH

I have flight
in my veins, ribs
which are feathered, fretted
like a wing.
It may seem I'm walking
with my head down or
it appears I'm running
clumsy, taking
the stairs breathy,
staggering short-limbed.
It appears
I'm tethered.
I tell you,
don't believe what you see,
what you think
you see.
I am winged
and breathing fire.

FIRE COUNTRY

Beginning with a line from Tarfia Faizullah's "West Texas Nocturne"

Because the sky burned, I had to unhinge
my sooty eyes from their lingering.

In the season of undoing, the tender heart-leaves
of the new are shredded

as soon as they arrive. Wind eats the view
and scalds a swath like a medieval dragon

as it moves across this land I've made
a home of. This is the land of the living,

despite what is buried here and the sand
with its urge toward erasure.

Everything is germinating,
and the horizon flares

with fires, distant and close, smoke
the color of sunglasses. I see

but my vision is skewed. Listen. I don't want
to sound such yearning but the wind howls too

and means nothing by it. The hills are on fire
and the desert is on fire and the air is thick

with other people's fires. And my own burning
is so small as to go unnoticed.

I am calling but the wind is busy
taking everything away.

BOMBAST

Always it's baby this,
baby that, spiraling through rooms and around
corners as if pulled on a string.
Damn all echoing voices and damn
elemental physics and wave theory. You can
forgo explaining all the world's rules—some of us
go along fine without knowing
how the refrigerator's motor manages to heat
inside but cool the air around it.
Just hear me out: I do
know that particles coalesce because
longing drives everything. I know
mussel shells hide their shine,
not-so-pretty on the outside and we
open them anyway,
pry into what is closed to us,
questing. We are
resolute, which means
stubborn. Tell me why we
think it all belongs to
us. We keep on breaking things,
voracious in undoing, then trailing behind
wailing like lost calves. Human
xenotype programmed for failure,
yearning, impatient, toddler species,
zeroing down our chances.

WHEN I AM TRYING TO BE HOPEFUL

We've passed the age of acid rain, angst-dream of my teenage years.
That river that burned in Cleveland

no longer catches fire. In the garden
the tomatoes are never bigger

than a thumbnail. The coneflowers
bloom pale, drooping their petals like nooses,

and trees that went bare
stay bare, the branches fingers of some cartoon Mr. Death,

grey and brittle, susurrating in the slightest breeze.
Say that was the dream

in which I was simply a bad gardener.
My other dream is all Technicolor blooming and bird riot.

The sun may or may not be more lethal
now and the television has stopped working

but the doors are open
and music is pouring in from somewhere,

loud and with a rhythm you can feel through your feet
as if the air itself is singing.

HOW TO SIT WITH IT

Look, the summer we walked up the river
there were bodies all around
not just the mud-flapped dogs shaking
their wet coats on the banks and not only
the other humans walking with their pants rolled up
carrying sandals or slogging
their water-heavy shoes through the current,
but there were fish that slid past ankles, just shadows
and touches like breath on an ear
and if you stood still long enough
a slight stinging, not unpleasant. We stood
in the speckled shade up to our knees,
watching children float sticks and throw slops of mud
for the splash, watching the dog paddle one side to the other,
step out and shake, paddle back. This was not before
either of us had lost anyone or had
those other kinds of griefs, those awkward pointed stars
there is no easy way to hold,
and I wanted to set mine down
just as I want to now, and I stood there
in the kind of varying light a good tree makes
on a shining river and I waited.

DEAR GRAVITY,

I know your voice. It is volcano-deep,
a rumble like a rhythm that is felt but not heard. Still,
it drops me. Wherever I am I feel you speaking through the gum-stuck walk
or the flame-orange hedge or in my tear ducts which let down their water
unbidden. What could be less convenient? I am always crying
in the naked sunshine. I blame you for reminding me
every hour to look down to where loss is kept.
The scattered leaves and, underneath, a bird's wing partitioned
into smooth grey fingers. My own hands swell and shrink
with the weather; how vexing to be made an instrument
that measures only what can't be mastered. I miss skipping,
though I could still do it. I miss that I could skip and feel the kind of alive
that made me dizzy so I would have to fling myself on the grass
with my head thrown back; the hum I felt there
a song I can almost recall the lyrics to.

WEATHER SYSTEM

There is wind on the stoop
shaking the door like the ghost

of our lost dog. In the inconsolable yard
green nubs have pushed up through the cold ground;

they turn in on themselves like people caught
in sudden weather, as we have been

sometimes on a mountain path, stepping under a burst cloud
and trying to make a shelter

from the curve of our own bent necks.
There is no end to it

while you are in it, the moving edges
take your own shape like a faithful shadow

while just down the valley you know the air is sweet
and still as a newly granted wish.

SOURCE

My child lived in a tree stump with his thousand brothers
before he came to us. When it was time to leave

the next in line would care
for the rest. He used to miss them

before the memory of them leaked away. Pregnant,
I dreamed him a kitten, dreamed him

a wild-haired girl, a drowned surfer
come back to live again. Today

I am thinking about cremation, how a body
surrenders to flames, arrives

as delicate ash someone might toss into wind.
My mother used to ask where her husband was buried,

but she has forgotten everything
she ever wondered; my sister has hidden his urn

where she won't accidently unearth it
while searching for a missing glove

or the right sized envelope. On the radio they are saying
how a body can be made quickly

into rich dirt to spread in your own garden.
Compost so hot even the bones break down. This is an afterlife

I can imagine. Before the illness
took his balance my father ran hills; it was

like putting on armor, or making a bargain
he believed he would always be able to negotiate.

There is an origami crane I was learning to make—
with every re-folding its crisp lines dissolved

imperceptibly, until suddenly it was no longer a crane.
However fast or slow the final burning

I like to imagine something of us returns
to that tree stump

where the unbodied live
in what used to be called their minds.

NOCTURNE

Car radio skims the room in which sheets
are already too much—
a splash of tin and static,
a heartbeat's slow stomp
beneath the floor,
the skin of the house shuddering
with work, all that water
in the pipes and behind my eyes,
running in the veins of trees
that shush at the windows.
The chair churns shadows
into the dream of a machine
that makes us
as sleep unmakes us, and in the next room
a boy with his arms flung up
to ward off unconsciousness
as he has always done—he fights
it, battles to stay awake
and then battles to stay asleep
as I turn once into sleep and once out of it,
rotating restlessness, shifting
ache to worry, worry to wish,
wish to dream, dream to the outlines
emerging and receding,
the motion of passing cars,
the forgotten light in the fish tank—
they will dart all night
small blue arrows
missing and missing their mark.

EVERYONE SAYS THE TRUTH WILL SET YOU FREE

Everyone says *This too shall pass.* Everyone says
Better this than the alternative.
I cart small vials of guilt and love, only the amounts
allowed in carry-on. I bring a change of clothes,
a good book to pass the time in waiting rooms.
I bring a steady hand. Some recipes.
I am only ever in time for the aftermath, never the moment
of crisis. I slow-step down hospital corridors
spouting cheerful banter. I shop and chop and throw
moldering left-overs on the down-low. I take recycling
to one canister, garbage to another. I throw out unneeded mail
and cracked dishes. I stay for only days. I am never
enough because nothing is enough because
everyone dies is not a helpful truth.
Because my company is partial
and my mind is elsewhere
and that sound you keep hearing
that is only for you
is the news that you are dying.

MAGICAL THINKING

I know we know no cure for this century
with its burning islands of trash, its traps of plastic.
On the sale table, a book of photographs is all brightness

and geometry, well-framed portraits of someone else's daily misery.
Yellow sheets hung on the line to look like sunshine
against a patchwork wall of dissipating mud. Beauty

fools me. I didn't want to wait for what came next.
I didn't see what was coming. I didn't ask enough.
Will these be the mantras of the next decade?

Because it's painful to know the truth
I eat little packets of seaweed
and imagine coral reefs somehow bubbled back

from ruin. Because wild poppies grow in sidewalk cracks,
fed on gravel and street tar, I carry hope on my hip
like a weapon I'm always ready to flash.

DEAR GRAVITY,

There are things even you cannot hold, objects
so light they evade your grasp, float
off leash in the sway of other forces.
Ashes are like this, and dust. And so in the end
it is wind that will carry our bodies away.
You may say it is all the same, a body in the ground
is just a slower storm. It comes down
to particles someone a century on might yet breathe
if there is anyone still breathing then.

*

I'm thinking about Caesar's last breath, that old math problem,
how they estimate each of us inhales
a molecule of him daily; some of everyone that's lived
lives on in the rhythm of our lungs.

*

Wherever his ashes are scattered, Gravity,
you won't be able to keep him still. Wherever
on earth there's breathing, he is.

ON SEEING A PHOTOGRAPH OF A TREE GROWING FROM THE SIDE OF A BUILDING

I, too, have been a stranger.
      Among the grocery store aisles
            of stacked colors, the necessary sorting
      of senses,   my face
in all the polished metal handles, grieving.
      One time F got me high
            and I drove us to the mountains
for miles, half an hour or
      a few minutes   before I noticed
            I was driving on the verge tipped
nearly sideways on the road's graveled edge.

ORACLE

The kestrel hovers in the barn's draft
      as if on strings, suspended while the mice grow accustomed
to the new condition of shadows, to the sense
      that something is there, above sightlines
waiting like a held breath for the moment of their forgetting,
      and they will forget, lulled by the day's stillness
and the grain dropped to the floor by the horses' careless chewing
      who are lazing now in the sun-struck field under clouds
that resemble wings and are filled with their own restlessness
      so that all is feather and sway
in the grasses, in the stubs of leftover stalks, in the shimmering
      top branches of trees so tall and far way
they are mythical, irrelevant beauties,
      while the air in the barn hangs like a storm
ready to drop its dark water, like a wire
      the moment before it is tripped.

ODE

Cuttlefish, my hero, my familiar
      the one underwater entity I envy,
the superpower I covet—
      on video I watch the magic show, morph
and disappear, translate
      from mollusk to rock to mere shadow
striped and stippling the ocean floor.
      There is dagger and tumble, how you scuttle
and obfuscate, ink cloud
      another darkness mimicking your shape. How I
have hidden,
      changed my colors in an eye-blink,
a mid-conversation conversion.
      How seaweed fronds
are mistaken for arms, while you are armed invisibly,
      mouthy, hungering, watching
as I am watching but with patience
      that seems infinite.

DEAR GRAVITY,

I must have breathed you in the post-storm air, the scent of ozone
lodged in me like those nanoparticles blanketing the ocean floors.
When I try to shake you loose, a little gale of lead bullets
swirls in the globe of my brain. You are a vision

I can't quite make out. Something like a ghost ship, or the cargo
I drop overboard, which keeps on bobbing to the surface,
which I keep finding again back in the hold, stacked this way and that,
with all the labels turned toward the wall.

PRAYER WRITTEN ON A WIDE VERANDA ON A COMFORTABLE COUCH IN SEWANEE, TN

If prayer requires an audience that is divine
and invisible, it is true that I don't pray. Better to say
I attempt to envision and hope to enact and perhaps
there is a German word for that,
one that sounds a little like a sneeze
and a little like a birthday-candle-wish.
Maybe what I mean is that I yearn or aspire
wishfully, wistfully, from anywhere I'm perched,
which happens just now to be amid a cloud
of French-fry-scented air in which a couple of butterflies
are spiraling and nearly settling on the rim of my tea cup
so that I fear I will sip them and so ruin their delicate wings.
I never wished to be a butterfly, exactly,
though something winged and barely-bodied might suit me,
suit how I am always floating loose from the weight and heartfeel
of my earthbound and bleeding form.
I have wished to leave my body entirely, like a cicada husk, whole,
translucent, empty and tenacious, clinging to some door's rusting screen
while another part of me got on with things elsewhere.
Other times I have imagined a substance, molten and seeping lava-like
into all the chambers of my body,
hardening to passageways I could then move through,
learn to slip the stubborn locks, discover
the short cuts and servants' staircases
and the colored glass windows hidden high in the tops of closets,
windows that flood with unexpected light so plush and dazzling
even the dust motes shine like ice crystals. How it would be
to feel myself a palace.
And I have wanted to be a tree, of course.
But I am a clumsy giant, always catching up gravel in my sandals,
uprooting tender stalks as I pass. Yesterday
a baby bird lay smeared and spreading into the dirt where I walked,
the ants already taking
the little body into the ground.
I am unprepared for the death of anybody.

My father says he is ready and unafraid; he wants to eat the world
and hold it in his pockets, has tried to memorize
its topography, its history and regional trivia, the equations
which attempt to explain its curvatures and potencies.
He collects what he can
even while giving away what he is no longer able to hold.
My mother is dropping the world like a trail of crumbs behind her. They disappear
before she can turn to look. There is no way back
and no view forward. She doesn't know she was ever carrying
anything. I know I can't control what matters
or most of what doesn't. I love the night moths
and the climbing vines. I even love a little the nest of yellow-jackets
waiting for the errant foot, the unseen dead thing betraying its last hiding
with stink, the lone leaf spinning and spinning where it has been caught
in a cobweb on a bicycle pedal. Insects rise up humming
from the grass where I step. I wish to be a hermit crab,
naked and rattling inside the beautiful shell of this world.

DEAR GRAVITY,

My father in his bed is a wrinkle among thin blankets. His breath
an engine turning over. His arms go up sometimes
in his ungentle sleep as if to protect the eggshell of his skull,
as if he is hiding under the desk of the world
and the sirens have begun to blare. Dear Gravity,
I cannot say he doesn't float, despite this heaviness.
He drifts in a half sleep, speaks
in a half tongue; such dreaming only the dying can do.
The meat he asks back to his bare bones
won't come from soup or cups of pudding
cajoled into the red gap of his open mouth which has gone loose
as a broken hinge. *One one one more only, this*
the very last, the nurse says, spoon tilted, her own hips straight
and solid, someone so planted in the world
it would take a violence to uproot her. My father
both sinks and soars in his dry thin paper skin.
His lips are red and dark despite their roughed up skin,
despite such poverty of moisture, they demark
the entrance to the watery cave of the body. The lexicon of questions
is poor in relation to that vast tunnel,
the red and slightly pulsing tunnel beyond the ivory markers
of his rotted, porcelain teeth. Where
in that disintegrating labyrinth
is the him that *is*? Not the lights that flash
and blink on the body's dashboard, not
the automatic systems that stutter along
until they don't. Not even the voice
that sometimes booms out orders
surprising the muddle of confounded mutters,
the litany of small refusals whispered hoarsely
in the direction of the lamp's plastic-wrapped shade.
What is left, Gravity, after the body has been turned to ashes,
and after his imprint and stink
have been replaced by someone else's and after,
even, the words have been spoken among
friends and family, and the catered panini cleared finally away,

after the urn has been placed on a mantel,
where will he be? Not anywhere
anyone's hand can reach for his own,
which rests yet on the blanket,
and through which runs a live blue vein like a mountain range at dusk
seen from very far above.

AVIARY

It was my mother who noticed
when his breathing stopped.
I was thinking of the hummingbirds

we had watched the year before, their throats
flashing among the feeders, how their commotion
woke my pulse. Now my mother

exited the bubble of her dementia
to say, as she had always done, the crucial thing.
The three of us had lingered on the porch, a bouquet

of small wings shimmering around us.
In the corridor where we waited while the nurses
did their work, my mother had already retreated

to other worries. In his last minutes
my father must have heard the flurry of our talk,
light laughter, his family enduring. Maybe

he was assured that he could leave.
Maybe the leaving wasn't painful.
He slipped from breath to death

so quietly. When we arrived
at the place where the hummingbirds were,
we didn't want to see our rooms. We wanted nothing

but to stay in the presence of all that urgency
while we held as still as we could.
He was never beautiful

but his mind was bright and quick and loud.
The hummingbirds, alerted by a signal
we couldn't know, ceased their whirring and were gone.

STAR DUST

*

And then somehow a slipping away, as if wanting no one to linger with you
at the door making plans for next time. You had come without a coat

so the leaving was easy. The door unlocked. You left
because it was late. It was raining

like it does in movies on bad days and you might have laughed
at that. It was late

in the morning and the hallways were busy with medication carts
and bodies practicing movement in their new realities. TVs, nurses, I assume.

I don't remember hearing any of it. There was a scientist
who measured bodies before and after death, I read,

to calculate the weight of the soul, and in the first minutes
you did look lighter. Later

there was gravity all over you,
how your body was sunk where it was, hardening.

Later I could hardly stand to look and would not anymore
kiss the smooth expanse of your forehead.

*

And when the funeral home people came
in their inconspicuous white SUV the rain had stopped

and we stood on the curb like newcomers
in the hard light of this strange land.

And my mother held my hand and did not ask what was happening.
And we went inside and eventually to lunch

where my mother whispered about a dream
in which her mother had died, her face stricken.

*

After a week a bracelet you had given me became you
and I began to whisper small reassurances to it

from time to time. Nothing changed really,
as it doesn't, as all the poets and songwriters and painters

already know it won't, though absence has a sound
like when the cicadas suddenly stop their droning

and the sky washes all that emptiness in. I name paint colors after it:
aftermath, lone cloud, shore between waves, phantom limb.

*

Grief is in you from the start and in you at the end
and though sometimes your days are flooded with it,

and sometimes your days are clear, we are made of it
as much as we are made of the ruins

of the first flaming star, whose far flung dust still spins
us into being.

TRUCK

Maybe I dreamed it: the doors open
like a mouth, a red light pouring out, the furniture skewed

like broken teeth. There were men
shooting framed pictures into boxes

as if they were basketballs. They stabbed
at conversation while wrenching the legs

from an oversized sofa. I'm trying not to speak
of regret or to make objects holier than they are.

No one said grief was any different thing than this
but now I know: it is seeing what someone you love once cherished

turned trash
at the hands of a stranger who can't help whistling.

DEAR GRAVITY,

On the trampoline my son and I try to bounce each other over.
We throw ourselves up to come down hard. We soar
until we fall laughing and breathless to the surface. We fail
to defy you over and over and that is the game.
We are bodies making room for ourselves in space,
pushing the invisible curtain out of the way. Nitrogen
and oxygen and the other vapors ricocheting madly
as I suppose they must always do. Everything I want is here:
the breaths I take easily and the purposeful displacement of matter,
my body feeling itself work and doing alright. A boy whose cells
are also mine. We will never win the game. We are dying
of laughter, and the light is fading, and the birds have started up
their evening prattle that I think must have something to say
about their allegiance to air even as they land and settle on high branches.

MANIFESTATION

Not even the paintings of Caravaggio prepared me
for the dead man curled like a kitten

and paler than dust.
There was no blood and the light was so thin. The closet

gaped and the buzz of hospital machinery
hung in the curtains like a left-over stink.

No one carried anybody else's head
away on a platter, though one nurse silently veiled

the bowl of uneaten applesauce. The plastic cup of ice chips
stayed un-melted

as if time had stopped in the room
while the hallway swirled with talk. Everyone is orphaned.

It is a secret club
the entire world is part of. Even my cat kneads the blanket

as if it is her own lost mother. The yard is full of little roadrunners
with no one to teach them

their dinosaur ways. All of the sights those eyes would have loved
are showing themselves off to someone else.

I will send myself articles that mention the word "poetry"
and books that are both academic and hilarious.

I will try not to think about the body, that rusted useless thing
that is always tripping on itself.

Maybe there will be hauntings, breaths
in the still air at significant moments, tea leaves

I will ask for advice. Maybe sometimes the shadows
will become doorways

I will strive to see you standing at the threshold of.

ACKNOWLEDGMENTS

Thank you to the editors of the following journals in which some of these poems originally appeared, sometimes in slightly different forms or with different titles:

The Baltimore Review
"Dear Gravity," [Shall I call you Shiva] and "Dear Gravity," [May I call you Grave]

Beloit Poetry Journal
"Dear Gravity," [My father in his bed]

Juxtaprose
"San Stefano"

Plume
"Latch" and "Prayer Written on a Wide Veranda on a Comfortable Couch in Sewanee, TN"

Poetry Daily
"Dear Gravity," [My father in his bed] [reprint]

Poetry International
"Prayer Written on a Wide Veranda on a Comfortable Couch in Sewanee, TN" [reprint]

South Florida Poetry Journal
"Oracle," "Chrysanthemum," "Ode" (as "Oceans 11"), and "The Last Falling"

Sugar House Review
"Fire Country" and "On Seeing a Photograph of a Tree Growing From the Side of a Building"

SWIMM
"Is That all There Is?" and "Tableau"

Tishman Review
"The Dress I Loved"

Verse Daily
"Fire Country" [reprint]

Thank you to my friends for support and cheer, especially to Nancy Mayer, my most tireless reader with her attentive eye and unfailing ability to call out my nonsense; and to Felecia Caton Garcia, Trish O'Connor, and Jennifer Jordán Schaller for inspiration, conversation, and making me laugh; to the CNM Writing Group, a weekly wild spark; to Sidney Wade for encouragement and vision and her dazzling poems, and to the Sewanee Writers' Conference for the community I found there. Thank you to my annual April Candles poets for their excellent prompts and for making a welcoming space for terrible first drafts, and of course for the delight of their poetry. Gratitude to Luke Hankins, editor extraordinaire, and to the crew at Orison Books for bringing this book into the world. And to Tim and Levi, always.

ABOUT THE AUTHOR

Rebecca Aronson is the author of *Ghost Child of the Atalanta Bloom*, winner of The 2016 Orison Poetry Prize and The 2019 Margaret Randall Book Award from The Albuquerque Museum Foundation, as well as a finalist for The 2017 Arizona/ New Mexico Book Award. Her first collection, *Creature, Creature*, won The Main-Traveled Roads Poetry Prize (2007). She has received The *Prairie Schooner* Strousse Award, The Loft's Speakeasy Poetry Prize, and The Tennessee Williams Scholarship to The Sewanee Writers' Conference.

ABOUT ORISON BOOKS

Orison Books is a 501(c)3 non-profit literary press focused on the life of the spirit from a broad and inclusive range of perspectives. We seek to publish books of exceptional poetry, fiction, and non-fiction from perspectives spanning the spectrum of spiritual and religious thought, ethnicity, gender identity, and sexual orientation.

As a non-profit literary press, Orison Books depends on the support of donors. To find out more about our mission and our books, or to make a donation, please visit www.orisonbooks.com.

Orison Books is grateful to Jessica Jacobs, Nickole Brown, and Renata Treitel for their financial support of this title.

For information about supporting upcoming Orison Books titles, please visit www.orisonbooks.com/donate, or write to Luke Hankins at editor@orisonbooks.com.